Dedicated to my Sister from another Mother

Copyrighted January 2025 by Linda L. Huff

THE BLUE PLANET

As I listen to all of the weather news around the earth,
I'm overwhelmed by the many earthquakes,
Tornadoes, floods, fires and mudslides.
Feet of snow and rain falling on top.

Have we gotten we only get ONE earth?
If we could all go into space and see
There is NO other place we could be.
Perchance we would understand that this is our ONLY land.
We should be trying to save it. Instead of enslave it.

And to those who think we would never sink so low. WAKE UP!
Climate change is here now.
The Garden of Eden is earth!
We should love it for all we're worth.
The native folk had it right.
Walk lightly through the world, respect all life,
Leave it better than you found it.

Don't cause stress or strife.
Or soon it won't be here for ANY
That we hold dear.

ROLLING, ROLLING

Eighteen wheels across the USA,
Running Nite and Day,
Bringing goods from coast to coast,
Trying to make the most of
The time and travel,
To bring people what they need:
From toilet paper, color TVs,
To cars and SUVS.

Seeing this great country on the ground
From town to town,
Meeting good folks and friends
Along the way.
Enduring all kinds of weather,
Lightning, thunder, rain, tornadoes,
Blizzards, fires and hurricanes.
Then there's earthquakes too!

Pack your nerves of steel
And hold tight to that wheel.
This job is truly a test
Of a strong-willed or crazy person,
Take your pick.
But no matter what,
This load must get there quick!

Talk on the CB,
Stop for fuel and a meal,
Call the "Travel Agent"
To get a new deal.

Chances are that everything you own
Was brought to you by those
Eighteen wheels rolling, rolling,
Across the USA.

Wind

Wind is one of the elements four.
With many, many names galore.
Mariah, El Nino, La Nina, Willow Wisp,
El Dreccho, Straight Line, and Inferno,
Just to name a few.

But by now I'm sure there is something new.
These words are used to describe something
You feel and see but can't touch.
And truth be told you wouldn't
Really like it much.

How can this ethereal element make itself seen,
Felt and heard when you can't touch,
Hold or keep it?

Wind also has these names bestowed.
Breezy, Gusty, Blustery, Gail Force and Hurricane.
What a force, what names.
I'm sure there must be many more,
But my fingers are getting sore.
So for now I say adieu,
To you and you and you and you.

RELOCATE

Let's move to Florida,
Where boa constrictors, pythons, alligators,
Water moccasins, cottonmouth, recluse spiders,
Scorpions, and hurricanes all abide.
Don't forget the cockroaches
Are the size of a small hummingbird
And can fly!

We aren't even talking about
The current political troubles.
Or the fact that ocean levels
Are on the rise.

The Keys will be the first to be underwater.
Wait and see.
As for me, I won't go there to stay,
But a visit is okay.

What will people do,
When living there is *too* cruel?
Where will they go when
The ocean takes their homes?

No answers have been made,
And I am afraid that no one
Is prepared for what is going to come.

So… Let's pack up
And move to Florida.
It could be fun!
A former Floridian.

VOLUNTEER

Volunteer when you retire.
It's so rewarding and you don't
Get mired in the same old rut.
Plus there is always something new to learn
As long as you don't keep your mind shut.

Skilled folks should teach or mentor a child.
If it's woodworking or being a welder,
Share what you know.
It will help both of you to grow.

Read to the elderly
And children too.
Both ages love a good story,
Wouldn't you?

EASTER IN MINNESOTA?

Well? Two days until Easter but you wouldn't know it.
Snow on the ground and wind blowing it.
Hard-to-find eggs of any kind in drifts of snow.
The Easter Bunny may need to ski, you know.
To bring back baskets of treats.
For all the kids to eat.
He will need his warm fur and maybe a coat.
If Easter was later he might need a boat.

The weatherman says hold on, it will get warm.
Soon baby animals will be born.
But till then we will have to deal
With wind, snow, and cold.
Maybe wait till it melts,
But frozen eggs will taste old.
Okay, okay, it's Easter in Minnesota after all.

WHAT IS MY PURPOSE?

Many of us ask
What is my purpose in life?
Sometimes our purpose
Doesn't show itself right away.
We roam around from day-to-day,
Trying to find just what
Our purpose might be, you see.
Oh my oh me, just what shall I do,
When I don't even have a clue.

Wait: I know now what I am here for.
I am a sounding board
For family and friends.
They call and tell me
About their struggles.
I tried to give some good advice,
And *always* be nice.
Even when I have heard
This complaint many times,
I nod and listen anyway.

Because I guess you see, I have
Found my purpose after all.
So if you are confused or troubled
Give me a call.
I'll try to help you solve
Some of your troubles, or all.
Even if it's summertime,
Or fall.

SUMMERTIME

Northern USA gets very happy
About summer time.
We can't wait to do the "ing" things.
Fishing, swimming, hiking, biking,
Canoeing, skiing, pontooning, tubing,
And don't forget 4th of July aahing and oohing.

It seems to go so very fast.
We always hope that it will last.
But no, soon summer will be in the past.
So get out there and do the "ing" things FAST.
Before the snow and ice of winter brings the cold.

WIND SPEAKS

Odd… How the wind sounds through the trees
With leaves and without leaves.
It's a much different sound
One from the other.
Makes me wonder:
How does the wind speak to trees?
And do the trees answer?
And if they answer,
What do they say?

OH wind, it was very warm today.
Or--OH Wind, please do go away.
Alas, we shall never know
If trees and wind carry-on so.

But it sure is fun to think they do.
Wind telling trees all about
Wind's travels.
That would be so totally cool.

AUTUMN

I'm always surprised by the fall season.
I'm never quite ready to let go
Of summer for some reason.
I need at least a week or so--no such luck.

Especially when I spy southward flying ducks.
Any day now, the hunters
Will be after those big bucks.
Halloween is on the way
And soon it will be Thanksgiving Day.
Oh my, Autumn is here now today.

COTTONWOOD TREES

Cottonwood trees in the fall,
Looking like gold coins in the breeze.
Standing in a copse of them,
Makes the very air seem almost golden.
Especially when viewed with the sky
That is a brilliant blue.

Kind of takes your breath away,
Also makes you smile.
What a gift to see
And hard to believe that it is *free!*

So… Go find some cottonwood trees
On a sunny day
And You too will feel the very same way.

Share this idea with someone.
Maybe even start a new trend,
To become a cottonwood
Tree-viewing friend.

UP NORTH

When you live at the top of the USA
Winter becomes very slow and very gray.
Not many days of blue sky and sun.
So whenever they do finally come,
We go kinds of goofy.
You might even say loopy.

Just to see the sun, and maybe
Go outside and go for a run.
Or at least get in a brisk walk.
We will talk to the people we are meeting
Instead of growling a greeting.
Faces will have smiles not frowns.
Children will carry on like clowns.

Just look what a blue sky and sun can do.
It lifts your spirits and your mood.
Bask in this wonderful day,
'Cause before you know, it will go back to gray.

MID-EAST

What is it about the Mid-East
Part of our world?
They have been killing each other
Since "before" Jesus came.
Just what would he say
If he came back today?

Life is hard enough
Without the fear of death,
Brought on by a neighbor.
Not only there, but everywhere.

We need to think
Before we speak, or act,
And that's a fact.
Then there is the golden rule…
Treat others as if they were you!

If that was in play,
It might save the day,
The people and the country too.

WEEDS

My friend says she's sure spring is here.
She has been in the yard pulling weeds out.
Pulling and pulling those nasty weeds out.
So many more to do, she has to shout
OUT OUT damn weeds, out.
Her back is sore plus there
Are so many more.

The front yard is done,
But there is more to come.
The back yard is calling for help.
So many weeds it can make you yelp.

So pull up your stool
And start pulling weeds like a fool.
And soon it will be
Completely weed-free.

TO THE CLASS OF '24

May you go forward into the world,
Armed with the knowledge you have earned.
Remember to be kind,
Even when others are not.
Though life may be fraught
With many trials,
Don't ever forget
To share your smile.

Be brave and true,
To others and to you!
Pursue your dreams
From car repair to sewing jeans.

Don't forget that many people
Are proud of you.
So go out there
And change the world.

HEAT WAVE

Sweltering heat, no rain in sight.
The temp at night
Is not delight.
My light bill keeps on an upward flight.

We need relief soon before we swoon.
Fans and AC are on twenty-four seven.
We are all praying to HEAVEN
That cooler weather will prevail.
But so far to no avail.

We seem to be in a huge hot bubble.
If it doesn't break soon
We could all be in trouble.

CABIN FEVER

I didn't really believe in cabin fever.
But after this winter, I'm no longer a dis-believer.
My cat has been driving me crazy.
Wanting to go out, but instead turning lazy.
Sleeping most of the day,
But running to the door to be let out.
I show her the snow is still all about.
She glares at me like it's my fault.

I bought her new toys,
To help her enjoy being in the house.
But she wants to chase a mouse
Or a squirrel, even a chipmunk would do.
Instead she's stuck in the house
And me too.

SPRING

Spring is here,
The robins cheer.
Tulips and daffodils are poking up
There and here.
Gardening can't be far away.
OH sunshine, won't you stay?

Rebirth, renewal, revive,
Spring makes Mother Nature live.

It also makes me want
To clean my nest.
To chase away that old pest
Winter.

Finally I think that
"Old pest" should be done,
Time to plan for summertime fun.

DROUGHT

Minnesota is in a drought.
Farmers are crying all about
That there is no rain for the fields.
Which will make very small yields,
Or maybe none at all.
We will have to wait till fall
To see if farmers can make it at all.

So rain come to stay,
We are needing rain today.
It seems only eastern USA
Has received our rain instead.
So please send it back this way.

Or we won't have grain to be fed,
For us, for cows,
For chickens and sows.

ONCE UPON A TIME

Once upon a time
Life was sublime.
No war or famine
Or weather gone awry.
No hate, jealousy or tears to cry.

Just where was this
Once upon a time?
In a book?
Or in a movie?
Was it a thought
Or a dream?

The answer has always been…
EARTH.
How you say?
Once upon a time,
And long long ago,
This was called EDEN.

Sadly we have stymied that notion,
Deeper than the deepest ocean.

DOG DAYS OF SUMMER

I'm melting, and melting,
I say with a grin.
But oh my, oh my,
Just where do I begin?

The heat and humidity
Are trying to be twins!
No air conditioning for me--
Not unless I want to sneeze.

So I have fans…
The electric kind,
To bring me a breeze.

I now know why
They call it the "Dog Days."
Because even a dog knows better
Than to go out in it.

THE NEVER-ENDING WINTER

If a Minnesotan was asked,
"How bad was the winter of 2022-2023?"
They will tell you in a second,
Believe you me!
Even the weather people were disgusted
About reporting that more snow
Was on the way.

Especially when the last four days
Felt just like summer days.
People were in T-shirts and shorts.
Everyone was talking about
Their favorite outdoor sports.

But then a Mother Nature reality check…
What the heck?
What a bummer,
No more summer?

Back to winter we go,
No No No!!!!

MAY DAY

May Day is only four days away.
We really hope to see flowers
And trees start to grow.
But winter's grip won't let go.
Cold and windy feels more
Like March instead of May.
Making folks want to say
"Where oh where is spring today?"

Is it hiding there under the earth?
Waiting for the sun to warm the turf?
Wanting birds and bees to come.
Soon… We hope.
And pray that spring
Will come to stay.

RAIN

Rain rain go away,
Come again some other day.
This is the song we are singing
As the weather keeps bringing
More and more rain.

We can't even enjoy outside fun,
Because we absolutely need Mr. Sun.

We are all hoping that we
Won't need kayaks and boats,
Or almost anything that floats.
If it doesn't quit
We might have a fit!

We were in a drought for the last three years,
But now NO ONE has those fears.

We hope and pray,
That maybe today,
It will be clear.

But by the look of the sky
It won't stay dry.
Oh me oh my,
Another day with more rain
On the way.
Glub glub.

FROZEN

We were buried in snow last year.
But this year it's almost clear.
Bitter cold is on the way,
But at least none has come today.

Maybe by Sunday we will see
An inch or two.
But the cold could turn you blue.
Everyone says that's okay.
We are hardy Midwesterners
We can jump into the fray.
But as for me I will stay
In the house tomorrow and today.

VISIT FROM A BUTTERFLY

Butterflies are really just
Flying flowers in the air.
They make you feel mellow and happy.
If I'm not being too sappy
They bring a smile to your face.
No matter when and where you see them,
Even if it's your neighbor's yard
Or your place.

To help them out, plant flowers
In your yard that they like.
Before you know
They will come and put on a show.
You will have the front row.

Fluttering, alighting and slowly flitting everywhere.
So enjoy a visit from a butterfly.
It's kind of magic when it happens
Because you see
They really are flying flowers.

NO TECH

I'm old-school.
I don't do high-tech.
People want my cell number
And my email.
I always tell them, without fail,
No CPU or cell phone too.

No one believes me.
So I have to tell them again.
The way they react,
You would swear you had just
Committed a sin.

But I don't need all that tech.
Please don't ask me again!

A TALE

If I wrote a book, it might look like a fairy tale.
Or maybe l would write about a whale,
With a very small tail.

Poor whale, he would have to work very hard
To get to where he wanted to go.
So perhaps I'll write about a very big toe.
It would have to be on a giant,
Who could be very defiant.
Because you see no shoe would fit.

Therefore, he would have a very big snit.
Or I could write about a dog or a cat.
Imagine that, a whale, a giant, a dog and a cat.
If I'm creative I could add a bat.

LONG DISTANCE

Long-distance grandparenting
Is a very difficult thing.
You are left with few choices,
Calling and writing
Are first on the list.

But nowadays texting and
Video-chatting are the best.
It is not the same as real life,
When grandparents can touch
And hug their grandkids.

Grandparents need the human touch,
Even though it isn't practiced much.
We know our grandkids have busy lives,
School, clubs, work, friends and sports
Take up their time.

But as long-distance grandparents,
We would LOVE for you
To drop us a line or two.
Or call.
You *could* call long distance, y'all.

LUCKY

We can count ourselves very lucky,
If we have a relative
Who is special.
The one who keeps it together
Even when it's falling apart.
Who is steadfast and true,
Who can navigate challenges
With an open heart.

And if you are lonesome or blue,
Will take the time to listen to you.
Who will encourage your plans and ideas.
And seems to know
Just how you feel.
Keep that person close to your side,
'Cause they are the family pride.

LETTER TO JESUS

If I knew the address to heaven,
I would write a letter to Jesus,
Begging him to come help us all!
Especially his "Chosen People,"
Plus everyone else!

How could I convince him to return,
When every day there's another horrible turn…
Of people killing each other.
Even down to fathers, brothers,
Sisters and mothers.
ALL for what??

Because you may have a different
Religious belief?
Get over it! Get along, cope,
Adapt, coexist!

We *are* all one race,
The "Human Race!"
If *only* I could get that message out!
Maybe I should SHOUT!!

So, as you see, we really
Do need your help! Really!

FRIENDS

I'm always surprised when
An old friend comes to call.
Especially when it's been years
Since I've seen them at all.

It's great to catch up
With life's ups and downs.
We laugh and cry
And sometimes frown.
We promise to keep in touch,
And not to let time go by so much.

Life is short, so keep your friends close by.
Because you never know when
You will have to say
The final goodbye.

SUMMER

Cicadas whirring, robins chirping,
House wrens warbling.
The smell of fresh-cut grass
Wafting in the breeze.
Sunshine and blue sky
Are here, too, please.

Hammock napping,
Beer uncapping,
Music hopping.
There is no stopping
The smells, sounds and sights,
Of summer days and summer nights.

The symphony at night
Is just so right.
Crickets and frogs
And sometimes even dogs
All join in.
It's quite a din!
But it's guaranteed to make you grin.
Summertime is finally in!

FARM GIRL

I was born and raised on a farm
In central Minnesota.
I'm the oldest of three.
When you live on a farm,
It doesn't matter if you are
A girl or a boy.
You learn how to take care of
Animals, gardens, housework
And of course time for a toy.

I watched and helped
Baby animals being born.
Learned about death and life,
And how to mourn.
Laughed and cried,
And always tried
To look on the bright side.
Learned how to milk a cow,
And how to ride.

I'm so thankful that I
Was raised on a farm.
It kept me safe
And far from harm.
It also taught me
Just how precious this earth is.

How thankful we should be,
To have this place to live and grow.
And to let our young ones know
To take care of our space.
It can only help
The human race.

SNOWLESS WINTER

This winter has been the winter
With no snow to speak of.
Which is been a nice change
From last year.
When we didn't know
If it would ever be clear.

Still cold from time to time.
But mostly the weather has been fine.
No one has to be a hero,
Because we have had temps
At 40° above zero.

As Minnesotans we know
That winter doesn't usually let go
Until March or maybe April.
And for those who love the snow,
There's always next year, you know.

COLORS

Orange, blue, red, yellow, purple and green.
Plus many more colors left unseen.
Periwinkle, violet and magenta,
Look what Mother Nature has sent you.

All the colors of the rainbow,
From ones we know, to shades we don't.
Even the lowly scums on ponds
Are very different greens.

So look around you
To see what can be seen.
You may be surprised by
What is right before your eyes.

Take the time to *really* see
All the colors that may be.

QUIET ONE

In almost every family
There is one person
Who has always been
Older than their years.

Even as a child they were fair,
Steady, quiet and strong.
Gently righting many wrongs.
Drying eyes that are leaking tears.
Listening to friends and foes about,
All of life's highs and lows.

On-call for the "Honey Do's" for
Relatives and friends near and far.
Even if it's just down the street
Or a hop in the car.
A quiet person who never
Toots their proverbial horn.

But you have <u>not</u> gone unnoticed
Since the day you were born.

SEASONS

This is the season of hot soups,
A good book, warm blankets and stews.
A change of outerwear has to come:
Parkas, scarves, hats, earmuffs,
Mittens and snow boots have to be on tap.

Inside you need: cozy bathrobes,
Fuzzy slippers, sweaters and a cat on your lap.

We tend to hibernate in this season
Of cold and snow.
Venturing out when we need gas
Or food to go.

We only go visiting
When relatives are in town.
We run from the house to the car,
Put the heater on high.
Wait with a frown,
Till it finally kicks in.

Wind so cold it will
Take your breath away.
Glasses fogged up,
Can't see, oh my oh me.
Wintertime is soooo much fun?
Maybe, when I was young!

DIA DE LAS MUERTOS

Day of the Dead,
It sounds very ominous and creepy.
But really, it's a celebration
Of people who are forever sleeping.
Memories of happy times, sharing stories,
Happy and sad ones.
Promises to one another
We are keeping.
Every year we will return
To the celebration,
And sadly may have to
Add one or two.
Regardless, celebrating them,
Remembering them
Is what we are meant to do.

So celebrate the
"Day of the Dead"
Don't let it go to your head.
Because you will be there some day too.

JACK S.

Okay, so you have been accused
Of not knowing "Jack Sh.t."
When in fact you don't really
Know him at all.

So let me introduce you
To some of his relatives.
Let's see… Oh, there's <u>Holy</u>.
He's a preacher.
<u>Ima, She'sa and Hesa</u>
Are sisters and brother.

<u>Who gives a</u> and <u>I give a</u>
Are first cousins.
<u>Tuff</u> is his uncle.
<u>Sacka</u> is his auntie.
<u>Youra</u> is his mom.

And we can't forget
<u>Hot</u> the stripper.
So now you know Jack!

H2O

Oh, H2O, how we need you so.
We can live for quite a while
Without any food.
But take away H2O
And things could get rude.

As you know, we humans,
Are made up of this H2O.
We need it daily
To live and grow.
All animals need it,
Even crows.

Without our H2O,
Plants, animals and human beings
Would soon expire.
We need to build a fire
Under our leaders,
To conserve H2O
No matter where it goes.

It's much more precious
Than any gold
That we may have or we may hold.

THE BEST

My mechanic is a star.
He's the very best by far.
If there were a metal
Or an award
For being the best,
He would have at least one a year.

So if your car, truck,
Almost anything on wheels,
Needs repair,
Bring it to someone
Who is very fair.

He treats your vehicle
As his own.
So… Give him a call.
Here's his phone.
864-3500.

RELATIVES

You can choose your friends,
But you are stuck with your relatives.
Some relatives are fabulous.
Some are hideous.
Some you wish weren't related.
Some make you feel elated.

Some come to stay and you wish
They would go away.
But of course you can't say
"I need you to leave so I can breathe."
They wouldn't be very happy
And could make your life crappy.

Some of them play head games.
Some of them never call or write.
A lot of them like to start fights.
Some you love no matter what,
Some you would like to cut out
Of your family tree.

But trust me, it won't work.
Besides, they would think
You were a jerk

WRESTLING GRANDMA

My Grandma loved to watch wrestling on TV.
It was black and white (no color).
She would pound on the arms of her chair
And holler. "Verne, get that Crusher,
Put him in a headlock. Don't let him block you."

Because of my Grandma I have to confess,
I also love wrestling. It helps me de-stress.
Even though I know most of the moves are not real.
It still brings me happy memories of Grandma
And how that makes me feel.

EASTER

Rejoice, repent, forgive,
Family, church, eggs, bunnies.
Celebrate the resurrection of Jesus.

But on the other hand…
War and famine in Gaza and Ukraine.
Who and when do we blame?

If Jesus came,
What would he say?
Could we change
Our horrible ways?
Why must we kill one another?
Instead we should be using our heads
To help each other.

EASTER: Forgive, rejoice, revive, live.

WAITING

I wait as you leave.
Look out all the windows.
And wait more. Take a nap.

Play with some of my toys.
And wait more. AHA!
Front door is opening.
No more waiting.
My human is home.

I am complete.

SCAMMED

I was sitting here today,
Wondering which bills to pay.
A phone call came.
They said my name.
Publishers' Clearing House
Was on the line.

I was very leery,
And said fine.
I really wasn't sure
That this was true,
And said so to Debra, too.

She assured me I had won.
But until the orange van
And Steve Harvey come,
I won't believe it until I see it.

While I wait I will pretend
The phone call wasn't the end.
I gave a call to PCH,
And they did reply:
It was in fact a lie.

I let them know all the info,
And PCH
Will shut these scammers down.

A GIRL NAMED SUE

We are lucky to say
We know a girl named Sue.
She loves dogs and cats
And loves to visit us too.

We play cards and fun board games.
Watch movies and eat great food.
We tell jokes and laugh
And those laughs put us in better moods.

We all need friends who bring us joy,
Whether they be a girl named Sue,
Or a boy.

HAIR MAGIC

Crystal is our hair solution.
She cuts, colors, washes and perms.
Even though sometimes we may squirm.
Always with a chat and lots of smiles.

She transforms us in a new way.
And when we pay we look like
A new woman as we walk out the door.
Who could ask for anything more?

BLESSED

I am very blessed.
All of my family are the best.
However, we do have one or two,
Who are in need of keepers.
When they are around
We open our peepers.

I have humorous,
Tech savvy, serious
And artistic ones.
Also slightly sneaky ones.

Some volunteer weekly,
Others sing in choirs sweetly.
We all get along,
So no fighting or drama.

We help each other out,
Even when we have to go
Find that darned runaway llama.

STATUS SYMBOL

I'm always confused by the folks
That think fancy vehicles and homes
Define who anyone is.

A house is just a place
To stay out of the weather
From day-to-day.

A vehicle is a way to go from point A
To point B without walking all the way.
I've never been impressed
By a car or a house.
Because both of them can also
Have at least *one* mouse.

It's sad to think that these "things"
Are used
As a status symbol,
And some use them to define themselves.
They miss the point
It's clear to see.
As for me I'm happy
Just being me.

THERE'S AN APP 4 THAT

It makes me wonder
If while we are downloading
All these apps
Aren't *we* being downloaded
Into the Internet?

Every time you add an app,
You give away a little more
Info about *you*.

So companies target their ads
To fit that info.
Too much is now on the Internet
For all to see.
Mistakenly, we believe
We are safe.
But alas we are NOT
At all.

Scammers and criminals can hack
Into your electronics,
One way or the other.

If not yours, then your hospital, school
Church, IRS or your bank.
Who do we have to thank?
Progress, I guess?

STATE OF THINGS

With Ukraine in a years-long
War with Putin,
And young people jacking cars
And shooting.
Then add crazy politicians,
Fake news and information.

I really wonder if our grandchildren
Will be able to live safely.
What kind of world are we leaving them?
They are the ones who will have to deal,
Yet some of you don't believe this is real.

But look around.
It's past time to sound
The alarm and no amount of charm
Will keep us from harm.

RECIPE FOR 100 YEARS

First, start with many years of laughter.
Half of that should be love.
Add half a cup of strife.
A quarter cup of small fears.
Sprinkle with a few tears.

Add dollops of hugs, facefuls of kisses.
A pinch or two of song and dance.
One teaspoon full of chance. (Optional)
Mix very well and let age.
Smiles are served on the side.

GETTING OLD

Getting old is not
For the faint of heart.
Some days are just fine.
But some days you can't even fart.
If you do, you should
Have been on the pot.

Peeing also becomes an issue.
Running to the loo.
At least once, maybe two.
Then trying to get back to sleep.
Aches and pains will no doubt
Keep you tossing and turning
For about an hour or so.

The weather also plays a part.
We now have built-in sensors
And good old "ART" will show up.
You slather on the hot rub.
You start to need help,
Like mowing the lawn
Or removing the snow.
Slowly, oh slowly, we now have to go.

No running around all day
And half the night.
Somehow this just doesn't seem right.

We used to have fun,
We used to rise to fight again.
And now, to my utter chagrin,
It's time to let *my* age finally *sink in!*
Yikes.

TRUE FRIEND

What is a "true" friend?
To be a "true" friend,
You must have <u>ears</u> to listen,
A <u>heart</u> to understand.
A truthful <u>tongue</u> to say hard truths.
<u>Patience,</u> even though you may
Have heard the story many times before.
Act as if it's just the first
Couple of times.

Be <u>welcoming,</u> no matter what
Time it might be.
<u>Loyal,</u> when someone needs help,
Do it where and when you can.
This is the path
To becoming a "true" friend.

LOSS

No words can express the sorrow
And loss you feel.
Only family and friends caring
And understanding can help you to heal.

The wondering, the questions,
The sorrow will remain.
All time can do is
Lessen the pain.

Hold onto all of the good memories.
Smile and laugh about these.
Those times will help you
Ease the pain in your heart.

ACCENTS

Ever notice that all across the USA
There are different sounds
In the way we speak,
Called accents by most.
It seems if you move
Coast-to-coast
Everyone knows where you are from.
All you have to do is open your mouth.

It's more noticeable North to South.
If you live there a year or so
You too will sound southern, y'all.
It's contagious and outrageous,
That our accent tells on us.

And we swear we don't have one.
That is until we hear one
That is different than our own.
Then by gosh, we do have one,
You betcha.
And go Vikings go!

ODE TO BILL G.

Mr. Bill has been our introduction to bling!
He sells us watches, necklaces, chains, rings
And all manner of glittery things.

Always with a smile and a joke
He helped us feel like un-ordinary folk.
We will miss his smiling face,
Plus no one else can take his place.
Rest in peace!

TRAINING

Jenny H. is going to be an Army MP.
She's training at Fort Leonard Wood.
Being the very best that she can be.
Let's keep her in our prayers and thoughts.
So she can stay strong and good.
We need young women in our Army,
Air Force and Navy.
Someone who can shoot a gun
And also say pass the gravy.
She's strong, smart and witty
But can be as gentle as a kitty.
So let's support her with calls and letters.
Which we hope can only make her better.

AGEING

Getting old is not for the faint of heart.
Most days you can go number two.
But be very cautious when you fart.
Or you and your underwear will part.

New aches and pains seem to appear every day.
So we put on creams and salves
We hope and pray will do some good.
We take our pills and meds.
It doesn't seem to take much food to be fed.
And boy oh boy we can hardly wait for bed.

Naps are also such a treat,
Sit back and put up your feet.
Do a puzzle, read a book.
Learn a new recipe to cook.
Make a call and keep a journal on it all.

Oh my, all of that just made me tired.
So bye for now
My bed is telling me to retire.

MY MOTHER'S HANDS

My mother's hands were there
To soothe, to calm, to pat me.
She let me play with them in church,
When I was little, to keep me quiet.

They baked and sewed, cooked and cleaned.
She spoke with them too.
She said she was part Italian.
Just her hands.
If her hands could talk
What a tale they would tell.
A life's worth of work and love
Encompassed into small things,
That were very large in loving care.

I love you, mom!

SISTER FROM ANOTHER MOTHER

My cousin and I are more like sisters
From another mother.
Always looking out for one another.
Sharing life's ups and downs,
From tears and laughter
To smiles and frowns.

Even though we were born in the same year.
I'm a much older woman than her.
By only months and a few days,
We often went our different ways.

But we kept in touch
Because we care about
Each other so much.
It's wonderful to me
That I have her in my life.

We are close as close can be.
Cousins by birth,
But sisters in our hearts we will
Always be.

THE ASH BUG

Oh, the sad sad day.
The emerald ash bug
Has come to stay.
Soon all 230 ash trees
Will be going away.

Which will leave our 'hood
Without shade of any kind.
That's not the *only* thing
That we will mind.

We can't even replant
Any kind of tree.
Which makes me very sad,
We are left bereft
Of the canopy we have had.

So… no help from the sun,
Which won't be fun.

Our park was so nice
With these trees, at least
60 years old and very tall.

What will we do without them all?
My gardens will also be under the gun.
My shade plants will now be
In full sun.
Which they won't like at all.

So I may have to change
Where they are.
But it will have to wait
Until next fall.

So sad, so sad,
I just feel so bad.
I love trees,
We need trees.

But no matter how much we beg
We can't make the city renege.
We are forced to deal
With no trees or shade.
Already it seems
Our fate has been made.

RENAISSANCE MAN

My dad is a real Renaissance man.
I happen to be his number one fan.
He's lived through the depression,
The dust bowl and World War Two.
He worked hard all his life,
And did have fun too.

He sang in many choirs
And put out many fires,
Real and metaphorical.
He really is historical,
Also very theatrical.

He can build a home,
Plant a field and bring
Pretty flowers to yield.
He gives the best bear hugs
And can also cut a "Mean Rug."

Gentle and strong
He doesn't ever do wrong.
I'm so lucky he's my dad.
Without him my life would be so sad.

WHAT A MINNESOTA BACHELOR FARMER LOOKS FOR IN A MATE

First, must like to hunt deer,
Pheasant and ice fish.
Able to cook same.

Second, must be funny
And smart.

Third, able to learn how
To operate farm equipment.
Fourth, must love animals.
So far, not many takers.

WINTER WOES

Frozen feet and toes.
A very red and runny nose.
Pipes that are froze.

Car won't start, cause it's
Colder than a polar bear fart.
Weathermen cheerfully report
We will have enough snow
To make igloos and forts.

The snow blower choked,
The handle on the snow shovel broke.
Machines and bodies need warmth
And hot toddies,
To deal with the winter woes.

LINDAISMS

I've been noticing that our "Minnesota Nice"
Is becoming harder to maintain.
Some may have lost it altogether.

Minnesotans are very nice
While you are visiting
Or vacationing with us,
Because we know that you will be leaving.

We are happy to see you come,
But happier to see you go!
Only Minnesotans can complain about
Minnesota, and do it any JUSTICE.

STINGER ENVY

When you can't tell the difference
Between a hummingbird and
A Lake of the Woods mosquito!

THE ART OF LISTENING

As a woman of a certain age,
I have finally perfected the "ART"
Of appearing that I *am* listening to you.
When in fact I'm making out
My grocery list.
This is indeed an ART!

RANDOM THOUGHTS

BUMBLE BEE

Hydrangea blooms are a
Bubble bath for bumblebees.
The way the bee works the flower.
First you see it, then you don't.
Like bubbles in a bath.

FARMSTEADS

Appearing as islands in a sea of corn.
Or as great ships passing in a sea of corn.

LEAVES

Autumn leaves in the breeze.
Looking like a blizzard
Of gold and red.
Following, twirling around my head.

LEAVES II

Leaves falling as a spring shower.
Running ahead of the wind.
Twisting, twirling, flying across the road.
Falling on the roof, sounding
Very much like a quick hard rainfall.
But it's only leaves after all.

FLOWERS

Flowers are a kind of magic.
It doesn't seem to matter
If you smell them or see them.
They can always bring smiles to faces
And take you away to your happy places.

www.ingramcontent.com/pod-product-compliance
Lightning Source LLC
LaVergne TN
LVHW010610070526
838199LV00063BA/5130